DOWNSIZE YOUR HOME RIGHTSIZE YOUR LIFE

DOWNSIZE YOUR HOME RIGHTSIZE YOUR LIFE

How To Cash In Your Home Equity &
Jumpstart Your Happy, Healthy Retirement

Sonya Myers

Small Town Publishing
PO Box 2146
Venice, Florida 34284

Copyright

ISBN: 978-1-889562-05-6

Printed in the United States of America
Photo of Sonya Myers: Patti Reed

Contents

Bonus Content

I'm constantly updating and supplementing the information presented here. Be sure to see the last section of the book for access to these valuable resources, including:

- Downloadable worksheets

- Information updates

- Book reviews

- and more

I suggest you skim through the book, download the worksheets, then return to complete the exercises with printed worksheets in hand as you read through the book more thoroughly.

Introduction

About 10,000 baby boomers retire every day. Roughly half of those who plan to move for retirement will downsize in the process, because for the average person a big family home is no longer needed. It costs too much to own and maintain, sucking up vast quantities of cash that could be spent on so many other things.

Consider this: the most significant expense for the working adult is housing, requiring roughly 30% of the average American's gross income. Add another 10% for commuting to work and a few more percent for appropriate clothing and meals out.

Do the math and it's easy to see just how much of your money goes toward keeping a roof over your head; almost half your income.

By drastically lowering your housing expenses when you retire, you'll be well on the way to enjoying a more fulfilling lifestyle. And if you own your home, there are additional opportunities to augment your savings, 401(k), and other investments as you downsize — an option many people overlook during traditional retirement planning. This book is for you, if you own your home and are open to the idea of living in a more sustainable fashion.

Instead of endlessly cleaning house or mowing the lawn during your off hours, you can spend time with friends and family. Instead of hiring painters or supervising a new roof installation you can enjoy hobbies and travel.

In short, you can simplify, decreasing your stress levels and increasing your enjoyment of life as you transition into retirement.

It sounds great, right? But the process can be overwhelming, with so many details and decisions to consider that it is often easier to do nothing. Especially if your friends and family resist your new path. But keep the faith, as many others have traveled this path before you. Let our experience light the way.

Downsize Your Home, Rightsize Your Life is a guide or roadmap for designing your most fulfilling life in retirement.

In this book, we explore how you can convert the equity in your home to cash, then spend a portion of the proceeds on housing while maintaining a high quality of life focused on your health and well-being.

To be clear, for our purposes equity is defined as the market value of your home less any outstanding mortgage or other financial encumbrance like a home equity loan or line of credit.

To make the most of your situation, you can use the remaining proceeds from your home sale to invest or even gradually draw down the balance to add to your Social Security or other retirement income.

In an ideal world, you are a happy, healthy empty nester who currently owns a home, with sufficient equity you can tap to fund or partially fund your retirement.

Through downsizing your housing and embracing a simpler lifestyle, you can continue to live the American dream. Whether you downsize into a smaller house, condo, villa, manufactured home, or even a boat or RV, by minimizing your housing you can maximize your opportunities to live the life you dreamed of during your many years of responsible adult behavior in the working world.

In the process, you'll carve out time to focus on your physical health through activities like yoga or bicycling or pickleball or belly dancing. Through the group experience and social aspects of these activities and other hobbies, you'll strengthen and maintain your emotional well-being as well.

You'll also have more time for your friends and family; time to visit children, grandchildren and dear friends. Time to enjoy the leisurely lifestyle you have anticipated for many years and to pursue hobbies and interests you filed away under "someday."

I call this lifestyle "rightsizing." Whether you prefer to put down roots by staying in one place for years, move frequently or even roam the world, living a rightsized lifestyle can provide much greater financial freedom than living in a traditional family home that is too big or used fully only on holidays or family occasions like weddings, anniversaries or birthdays.

When you sell that money pit of a house (or to put it more kindly, your long-term forced savings plan) you can use the proceeds to cut your living expenses dramatically.

Imagine the life you can lead when you're finally free of the ongoing expense of an oversized property that demands all your time and most of your money to clean, insure, and maintain!

By investing some of the proceeds in a smaller home, you can and likely will pay less in property taxes and insurance fees. Your utility bills will be lower. And if it's a newer home you'll enjoy even greater savings due to increased efficiency of construction and lower insurance rates.

One thing to keep in mind is that all homes and communities are not created equal. There are a number of factors to consider when designing your own personal rightsizing transition. Among the most important are:
- Location and climate
- Type of home
- Culture of the town, city or community
- Community fees, amenities and restrictions

That's the short list. There are many decisions to consider when finding your perfect situation, and each person's criteria will be different.

Retirement is like a three-legged stool. It requires the balance of finances, health, and emotional well-being. If one leg of the stool is weaker than the others, the stool is out of balance and will certainly wobble, if not actually fall over.

One of the goals of this book is to show you the big picture of a balanced three-legged stool, so you can define what a successful retirement looks like for you. In addition to laying out the financial benefits of tapping your home equity, I help you figure out who your new "tribe" of friends and associates are — those who enjoy the same activities and pastimes as you.

I also encourage you to focus on your health, because health challenges have derailed many a retirement plan.

Of course, we'll also look at various options in housing and communities, the financial component so critical to the rightsize formula.

Finally, you'll gain access to a series of worksheets to help you clarify your prospects and preferences so you can develop a personalized plan for your retirement.

With some simple math, defining your likes and dislikes, and then researching specific communities and homes, you can create an action plan to move you along the path toward living your dream.

But first, here's my story.

Chapter One
My Story

My husband and I have owned 12 homes in the last 20 years. Large homes, small homes, remote homes, town homes. We've owned property in three different states as experienced serial home owners who never stayed put for long, always looking for that next adventure in a new house and a new community.

Our most recent home – which we called the Alamo for the huge stuccoed archway of a gate across the driveway – was fairly large for Florida. On almost two acres, it had three bedrooms, three baths, formal living and dining rooms, a huge kitchen, a pool, a detached art studio, and RV parking.

We stayed there for almost six years. But after yearning for less responsibility and more freedom for the last two of those years, I finally hauled my husband on board. I walked him through the math outlined in the next chapter, then showed him a few houses in the community I liked.

As a real estate agent, I see a lot of communities and houses. It only took 24 personal trips to the closing table before that particular light bulb went on and I got a license in Florida. (For each purchase, there was also a sale. Twelve homes equals 24 closings.)

My husband wasn't that impressed with my top choice until we toured the community center, workout facilities, library, pottery studio, and pool.

Those amenities, plus being within walking distance of a grocery store, several restaurants, the town library, medical resources and downtown, finally convinced him. It was time to let the Alamo go.

The entire process – which included researching options, de-cluttering, fixing up, estate sales, staging and selling the old house, and buying the new one – took about six months. We bought the new place in April and listed the Alamo in August. It sold in September.

Here's a scenario for a similar situation, using numbers from sellers I recently assisted:

Home Sale & Purchase

Net proceeds from sale: (after paying sales commission)	$340,000
Cost of new home:	$225,000
Cash balance:	**$115,000**

Monthly Overhead for Old Home

Average electrical:	$175	
Water/Sewer:	25	
Cable/Internet:	225	
Lawn care:	150	
Pool care:	80	
Taxes & Insurance:	500	
	Total:	**$1,155**

Monthly Overhead for New Home

Average electrical:	95	
Water/Sewer:	25	
Cable/Internet:	60	
Lawn care, HOA:	90	
Pool care:	0	
Taxes & Insurance:	300	
	Total:	**$570**

Monthly Savings:	**$585**

Multiplying the monthly overhead of $1,155 by 12 to get a yearly figure equals $13,860 for the old home.

$$\$1,155 \times 12 = \$13,380$$

Monthly overhead of $570 times 12 equals $6,840 for the new home.

$$\$570 \times 12 = \$6,840$$

That's a savings of $7,020 every year.

$$\$13,382 - \$6,840 = \$7,020$$
(or $585 a month)

So by rightsizing their living arrangements, this couple freed up over $115,000 in cash and an additional $7,000 a year. If actuarial tables are anywhere near accurate and they live another 20 years that $7,000 adds up to $140,000 without considering re-investing it or the impact of inflation. By my simple math they saved about a quarter of a million dollars by rightsizing their real estate.

Robert Stammers, director of investor education at the Chartered Financial Analyst Institute (CFA), suggests that if half of your net worth is tied up in your home, maybe it's time to reallocate some of those funds and balance your portfolio.

You can re-invest some of the proceeds or use them for living expenses or treat yourself to travel or fulfill other long cherished dreams.

Please don't think this strategy works for only one scenario. You might have extensive holdings in a family trust or your retirement accounts and wish to preserve those assets for future generations. Or you might have very little equity in your home.

You can easily adjust the simple formulas in this book to fit your situation. There are as many reasons to rightsize as there are readers of this book. And there is equal opportunity for everyone to decrease overhead in pursuit of a more fulfilling lifestyle.

My friend Janice oversees a family trust. She has just begun the process of rightsizing by researching the type of home that will suit her needs after she sells her sprawling estate home. Janice will then buy a less costly home and spend some of the remaining proceeds traveling the world. The trust fund remains largely intact for her children.

Last year, I helped Joy and Larry find a home

in a nearby town. By selling their previous home and a small furniture company, they were able to retire in a modest home with plenty of disposable income to pursue their passion of kayaking the inland waterways of the Gulf Coast.

What about you?

What's your dream retirement? And how can you afford to live it? To get started, consider how much your current home is worth and what it costs you to maintain or "carry" it.

Then calculate your net worth and use that figure as a starting point to design your new lifestyle.

Along the way you'll give a lot of thought to how you spend your money now and how you will spend it in your retirement. Each area you examine and adjust will reveal additional ways to reallocate your retirement dollars. It all adds up to a more fulfilling bottom line for the next phase of your life.

Are you ready? Let's design your new life.

Note: When you sell your primary residence, IRS guidelines currently allow you to keep up to $250,000 of gain or profit tax-free if you're single or up to $500,000 if you're married. That money can be an unexpected windfall in retirement. As always, certain rules apply for this preferential tax treatment. But typically, if you've lived in your home for at least two of the last five years, you can qualify for this tax treatment. Consult your tax professional for more details.

Chapter Two
Design Your New Life

Are you excited about this once in a lifetime opportunity to do exactly what you want with your life? I hope you share the enthusiasm I am enjoying as I look forward to the first mild beach-side season in my life where I am totally in control of my time and talents.

Your enthusiasm will help sustain you throughout this process, too. There will be challenges. It's not all rainbows and unicorns. My training and experience as a life coach helped me tremendously as I worked through the many thorny decisions and resistance issues that cropped up while letting go of the house, possessions, and frankly, some long held dreams like raising miniature donkeys and planting a bamboo farm. From time to time I called on other coaches to help me through the rough patches.

But now the big house is sold, the little house is fresh and organized and the future awaits. Here's a step-by-step list I developed as I went through downsizing and rightsizing, just for this moment. Use it to help you focus, gain clarity, and stay organized. It's a little tongue in cheek, because at this point we can afford to be playful, don't you think?

Step 1. Give up the small stuff first

One new normal you will face in retirement is this: few people care what you did prior to your retirement. If someone requires your bona fides before befriending you, is that really someone you want in your new circle of friends? More likely, you'll be asked where you're from, not what you did in your career.

In retirement, you're on equal ground with your peers. Unless of course, you have the means and desire to pursue an exclusive, country-club lifestyle that requires considerable financial resources. In which case, you may be reading the wrong book, right?

While it may come up in general conversation,

the bottom line is that people who are retired are more interested in what you're doing today than what you did in the past. That big corporate job you or your spouse held? People don't especially care. The vast wardrobe of business and otherwise dressy attire, you can donate or sell on eBay. It will just take up valuable storage space in your new digs.

In this new phase of life, you'll most likely dress in casual clothes. You might keep a few more polished outfits if you volunteer or attend functions that call for something other than a pair of shorts or yoga pants and a t-shirt. But it will not be unusual if you pare down the wardrobe to the point where your closet holds only a couple of weeks' worth of casual clothing.

One reason consignment shops and thrift stores abound in retirement areas is the desire newcomers have to downsize their wardrobes. Many go through this process several times and some people even have a one-in, one-out policy to prevent clothing creep.

The benefits of a streamlined wardrobe are many: fewer decisions to make about what to wear, less expensive to buy and maintain, and saving time and energy by shopping less. There is more than one movement built around this process, but perhaps the most well-known is Project 333, the minimalist fashion challenge that invites you to dress with 33 items or less for three months.

So prepare to go through your wardrobe more than once, eliminate more clothing each time your thinking on this topic evolves.

Step 2. Create an inspiration board

If you haven't already, starting clipping photos, quotes, infograms, and other graphic representations of the life you want to live in retirement.

Attach these to a large surface where you can see the board daily. You can collage elements to a poster board or canvas, pin them to a bulletin board or tape them to a wall or unused door.

A handy way to carry your inspiration board around with you is to take a photo of it with your smart phone. You can even make a screen-saver of the image to remind you of all the goals you're setting and the experiences you hope to enjoy.

If you're more traditionally organized, create file folders for various categories like contacts, communities, destinations, budgets, asset and liability lists, etc.

Step 3: Simplify

Begin to consolidate your bank accounts where it makes sense. Pay off small outstanding bills and think about reducing the number of credit card accounts you keep open.

Get off email lists for groups you no longer participate in. Unsubscribe from email newsletters that no longer interest you. Cancel subscriptions to trade journals or work-related magazines that you just don't want to read anymore.

Step 4: Get technical

If you don't already have one, get an email address that is universally and easily available, like your-firstnameandlastname@gmail.com.

With a free gmail account, you'll be able to access your email from virtually any computer where you can log onto the internet, anywhere in the world. It's easier to keep in touch with friends, family and even pay your bills online from one common address. Also, you can simply forward your old email address to your new one, if you like.

Or take the opportunity to cut back on the number of people you communicate with by simply starting fresh and reaching out to only those you want to stay in touch with.

Step 5: Diversify

Do you have sufficient interests to sustain you in retirement? Hobbies, volunteer work, social groups or a part-time job? If not, start to cultivate these interests now so you'll have some structure to rely on when you retire.

A relocation and/or retirement often brings an abrupt halt to routines, but if you have a safety net in the works the transition will be a lot smoother and more pleasant.

Step 6: Be open to possibility

Plans and dreams are good, but don't be too rigid. Pay attention to the little whispers you hear from your inner self.

Follow your intuition and allow yourself to investigate topics or experiences that attract you, without worrying about the time or energy you're investing without a guaranteed return.

This is a time of experimentation and exploration. Your priorities are changing, heck your body is changing, too! It's a little bit like being a teenager again.

Dare to step into what interests you. If not now, when?

Questions and answers

Here are a few areas of inquiry to further help you envision your best life after retirement.

It's helpful to write down the answers, and repeat the exercise periodically throughout your downsizing and rightsizing journey. Your ideas about this new life will evolve and grow more precise as you examine your options.

Retirement is a vast sea change, involving new discoveries as well as loss and grief. How do you feel about losing or replacing the following relationships?

- Your old house (yes, it is a relationship!)

- Your favorite neighbor

- Your least favorite neighbor

- The path you walk around your community

- The place you work out

- Your closest friend

- Your least favorite person
- Your job
- Colleagues from work
- Your place of worship
- Doctor(s)
- Hair stylist
- Favorite restaurant
- Grocery store
- Mechanic

If you use a journal to complete this exercise, you can refer back to it later. If this is your first experience with "journaling" you might be surprised when you reread your journal, later in the process.

What do you hope to enjoy about the new relationships and activities you plan to develop? Here are a few elements to consider.

- Art center
- Travel agent
- Religious or spiritual contacts
- Clubs or organizations
- Learning institutions

What have you always wanted to do or learn?

- Sing in public?
- Play an instrument?
- Make pottery?
- Paint?
- Write a book?
- Make jewelry?
- Design light fixtures?
- Develop an app?
- Mentor someone?
- Volunteer your time?
- Learn to drive a boat?
- Travel in an all-female RV caravan?
- Visit a foreign country?
- Learn to fly?
- Become an Uber driver?
- Camp in the wilderness?
- Hike the Appalachian Trail?
- Visit all 50 states?
- Take up woodworking or mosaic building?

- Read Tarot?

- Train dogs?

- Get in shape?

- Take a solo trip?

- Design your own typeface?

- Rob a bank?

What is the most outrageous and scandalous thing you have ever been tempted to do?

If the answer is unrealistic or just plain nuts, how could you get the same feeling, without actually doing that outrageous, scandalous thing? When you have an answer to that question, be sure to write it down for later consideration.

Now dream it

By now you should have some interesting ideas for how to expand your life experiences. Take a few moments to visualize yourself doing any one of the items on the list that made you laugh out loud or caused a sizzle of excitement to travel up your spine.

And repeat

The more you can imagine yourself participating in your dream activities, the more of that good feeling you'll get. Plus, you're practicing for your actual ideal life!

It will help you immensely to keep your dreams and desires close and accessible. Look at your visual representations and lists often, daily if you can.

Retirement is one of life's major transitions and you may experience just as many lows as you do highs. Be prepared to go through both.

One thing that will help you weather the transition and make the most of your retirement is good health.

Chapter Three

Health & Well-Being

You've heard it countless times; heart disease is the number one killer of mature adults in America. Two huge factors in preventing cardiovascular disease are your physical and emotional health.

A healthy mind and body are critical to your successful retirement. In addition to lowering the risk of heart disease, many experts now believe exercise helps prevent diseases like cancer, diabetes, and Alzheimer's, and provides relief for conditions like arthritis and depression.

In 2017, the National Institutes of Health (NIH) will launch a huge six-year study of 3,000 people. The goal: to prove that exercise is medicine. The results may change the entire fabric of our health care industry.

Current guidelines recommend 150 minutes of strength and cardiovascular physical activity per week. Sadly, more than half of all baby boomers report doing no exercise whatsoever. If you're among them, please commit to change your path right now.

Here are a few suggestions to begin or strengthen your physical and emotional well-being. Some you have heard before, but now that retirement is within reach it's time to take them to heart. Pun intended.

Get active

There are so many physical activities available in today's world that it just makes no sense to be a couch potato. If you're planning to retire in a warmer area like Florida or Arizona you will be amazed at the number and variety of classes and solo options out there.

Even if you're in a small town or a rural area you might be surprised at the classes or informal groups available to you. If there is nothing, why don't you start something?

A surprising niche part-time job for Boomers is fitness instructor. Have you ever attended a class taught by a younger instructor who either didn't know or didn't care about special needs or physical limitations of students in the class? This attitude, born of youthful ignorance and self-absorption, is all too prevalent in the fitness industry.

There is a growing need for mature instructors, especially in retirement destinations. A bonus is the incredible level of fitness you can attain as an instructor. I experienced this phenomenon the two years I taught yoga and Pilates. Although I rarely completed a full workout myself, the constant motion and ongoing demonstration of moves took me from a size 14 to a size 10 during that time. And I only got sick once, due to a student who came to class suffering from a contagious form of bronchitis.

As with any profession, there are excellent and not-so-excellent practitioners. Be very discriminating about who you choose to trust with your body. Getting in shape doesn't have to hurt and instructors who subscribe to the "no pain, no gain" theory are just plain wrong.

Here is a list of possible activities for your consideration:

- Yoga
- Tai Chi

- Pilates
- Walking
- Hiking
- Biking
- Dancing (from ballroom to belly)
- Tennis
- Pickleball
- Swimming
- Water aerobics
- Kayaking
- Paddleboarding
- Weight training
- Roller skating
- Bowling

In addition, a mind-boggling array of indoor classes can be found at your local YMCA or gym. Your goal here is to work out at least three times a week, with a combination of stretching, strength training, and cardio exercises.

Out of shape? Start where you are. Bad knees? Take a chair yoga or chair dance class. Yes, both are a "thing" and will get your heart rate up and the sweat flowing.

Just be sure you have your doctor's clearance, especially if you have health issues. He or she should be able to recommend suitable activities based on your level of fitness and any limiting injuries or conditions. And find an activity you enjoy, so it will seem more like play than work.

Eat smarter

This is a tough one for almost everyone. You know what helps? Hanging out with people who already eat smart. Positive influence, free of charge.

If you need the support of a dietician or health coach, please arrange for that service. By improving your health, you will pay for this seeming luxury in the form of reduced health care costs in the long run.

In coming chapters, you'll see how much money you'll save by reducing household expenses in the rightsizing process. Getting healthier is an excellent hobby to embrace as it directly impacts both your bottom line and your retirement experience.

Make friends

Finding your tribe at the yoga studio, or wherever you spend time, is the foundation upon which you will build your healthy new life.

Your workout buddies, even if they are casual, will motivate you to suit up and walk out the door when you might not really feel up to it. Really, who likes to work out? Who looks forward to pulling on the snug workout wear and possibly looking silly in front of other people?

Sadly the tradeoff, that positive effect of physical activity, is felt only when you actually move your body. Reading the book or watching the video won't cut it. You must actually engage! Then the endorphins start to flow and you wonder why you ever hesitated in the first place. Not only that, but the effects go far beyond the immediate endorphin high.

A recent study published in JAMA found that of all the options available to prevent back pain, exercise is the only one proven to work.

Researchers reviewed more than 6000 studies on back pain prevention and found that exercise along with education reduced the risk of back pain in the coming year by 45 percent. If you've ever suffered from back pain or nursed a loved one when their back went out, that should get your attention.

Back to the tribe argument, scientists are digging deep into the reasons why the health-damaging effects of loneliness appear comparable to those from smoking, diabetes and obesity. Basically, they are looking for the link between social isolation and cellular changes that lead to inflammation and depressed immune function.

The critical importance of your tribe
Cultivating or establishing community is critical to your physical health and emotional well-being. Introverts, extraverts, ambi-verts... we all need our peeps.

The bottom line is that lack of community has a profoundly negative impact on your health.

In 2010 researchers at Brigham Young University reviewed 148 studies of over 300,000 people on social relationships and mortality. They found that the stronger a person's social relationships, the higher their odds of survival – nearly 50 percent higher in the best-case scenario. That's an increase equivalent to stopping smoking!

Researchers believe the connection between

friendships and health is found in how the body processes stress. Isolation increases the kind of stress commonly called "fight or flight" which keeps us safe from marauding beasts but is not designed to power our systems on an ongoing basis. It causes too much wear and tear on the body, which leads to illness, injury, and disease.

Yang Claire Yang, a sociologist at the University of North Carolina, Chapel Hill, studied the health effects of friendship by comparing biomarkers such as blood pressure, body mass index, waist circumference and levels of the inflammation marker C-reactive protein.

Of interest are the specific results on participants in "old age". Those with a lack of social connections exhibited more than double the risk of high blood pressure, raising it by a whopping 124 percent.

Overall, the latest research indicates that having quality friendships is just as beneficial as exercise. Combine friends with actual exercise and just imagine the impact!

Quality is the key
Other experts emphasize that good relationships are good for you. Contentious

relationships, not so much.

Blood pressure shot up for those engaged in positive relationships with negative aspects. An example might be when you love your mother, but she is overly critical or otherwise not supportive.

Surprisingly, participants found it less stressful to deal with people they outright disliked than with those they had positive feelings for, but difficult exchanges with.

It seems that a greater number of good friends improves our health.

All this to say, if you're going to invest time and energy into rightsizing your life, start now to improve your mental and physical health to the best they can be. Doing so will help you ease into the transition with less stress and anxiety.

Wondering when we'll get to the nitty gritty details of finance, downsizing, and best places to retire? That's coming up, in the next chapter.

Chapter Four
What Are Your Assets?

The first step in deciding how much money you'll have to work with is to calculate your net worth. Net worth is the value of your Assets minus your Liabilities or debt.

If you've read this far, your biggest asset is very likely your home. According to U.S. Census Bureau data released in 2015, the typical American's net worth at age 65 is $194,226. However, removing the amount derived from home equity results in that figure sinking to just $43,921.

In other words, not including the money tied up in the house, the average American has $43,921 in assets. Converting the house to cash would make an additional $150,305 available for alternate housing or investment.

That's a shocking imbalance of your investment dollars. And a potentially valuable resource for your retirement.

Although they probably pale in comparison, your other big ticket assets might include cars, boats, RVs, or even airplanes.

In addition, you probably own an assortment of artwork, furniture, and jewelry. Maybe you have valuable animals or hobby equipment and supplies. Anything that is physical and can be converted to cash is considered an asset.

To calculate your net worth, begin with your biggest asset, your home.

Although you might think the value stated on your home owners insurance policy is a good place to start, that figure could be outdated. There are two better ways to get an accurate estimate of your property value: an appraisal or a market analysis by a Realtor.

The easiest, fastest and most economical path is through the real estate community.

Market Analysis

If you don't know a Realtor you trust, here is how I suggest you begin. Pick three different local real estate brokers or companies. In addition to independent brokers, your community probably has an assortment of franchises like Coldwell Banker or ReMax.

Pick out three that appeal to you, but don't over think it. If you like their ads, descriptions or overall designs, just go with your instincts here.

Then call the managing broker of each firm, one by one. Tell them you are interested in a market analysis, as you're contemplating selling your home. Ask them to suggest an agent with these attributes:

- three to five years of experience

- completed at least five transactions in *each* of the last two years

- has in-depth knowledge of your neighborhood

As a Realtor myself, I believe this is the sweet spot with agents. This group contains those who are new enough to be enthusiastic and also have plenty of time to devote to you. They have helped enough buyers and sellers through the process to have a good grasp of the details, which requires a certain level of competency that can only be gained through experience.

If you live in a small town or rural area where the number of agents is limited, you can always look in the nearest large town. I've used this tactic before, with success.

Under no circumstances should you sign a listing agreement with any of these agents until you have seen all three reports and spoken in depth with each of them.

Many sellers are tempted to go with the highest number they are presented, but this can be a costly mistake. When an agent takes a listing that is priced higher than recent sales figures support, it is called a "vanity listing" or the agent is said to "buy the listing."

Which basically means that pretty For Sale sign in your yard is free advertising for the agent and she's fine if it stays there for the length of your agreement. Pricing to sell is the way to go if you're serious.

If your home is priced right and the market is active here is the painful truth: you should get multiple showings within the first week and be under contract within 30-45 days. National statistics indicate that most activity takes places in the first three weeks of putting your house on the market. After that, showings drop off to almost nothing.

If your house is over-priced you will lose the best opportunity you to have expose your property to the largest number of potential buyers in that critical three week period.

After 30 days with no offers, your agent will probably ask you to reduce the price, and encourage you to keep reducing it until the right person happens along to buy your house. The purchase price will very likely be lower than if you had accurately priced it in the first place.

When you over-price, you stand to lose not only money but also your valuable time. So price your house competitively. If you have any hesitation about which of the three agents to choose, interview three more. If you still haven't found your agent, you're probably procrastinating. Just sayin'.

Appraisal
If you have a bit more time and are willing to pay a few hundred dollars, you can get a formal appraisal. An appraisal is a more exact calculation of value, taking into account a

number of measurable factors. Hire only a licensed and certified appraiser.

To find appraisers ask local banks, mortgage brokers, real estate attorneys or your accountant for recommendations. Again, interview more than one and be sure to explain that you need a value for the purpose of selling your house.

The only caveat here is to avoid the local "deal killer" appraiser. It seems like every market has one, the appraiser who consistently undervalues property, effectively destroying sales that involve a mortgage and seriously undermining the entire system.

For whatever reason, these individuals seem to resent it when prices rise as real estate appreciates and reflect that attitude in their work. Avoid them by simply asking your sources who they would avoid as well as who they recommend.

If your property is unusual in some way, it may be a good idea to pay for an appraisal rather than depend on the real estate market analysis, which depends on recent sales of similar properties to establish value. Without those, a Realtor is making an educated guess as to the value of your outside-the-box property, while an appraiser has more tools at his or her disposal.

Once you have a value for your home, start writing a list of assets or create a document on your computer, noting the amount under the heading Assets: House.

Turn to the end of the next chapter for a sample Net Worth sheet. You can download that and other worksheets from my website at:

sonyamyers.com/insiders

If you own other real estate, go through this process with each property and add the figures to your Assets.

Remember, we're looking for the overall value of your real estate, not considering how much you may owe if it has a mortgage, line of credit, etc. That step is covered in the next chapter.

Cars, Boats, RVs and Airplanes

Estimating the value of your other major assets is a much simpler process than estimating real estate values. There are books and websites available where you can look up your exact make and model to get what is commonly referred to as the "blue book" value on your used vehicles.

The original Kelley Blue Book was developed

to help banks and insurance companies value vehicles for their respective needs. Today, there are several similar sources you can use to estimate the amount a dealer would give you on a trade-in or the retail resale value you can expect when selling privately.

If you have the original sales paperwork on your car, this process will be a lot easier. The features and upgrades listed there are a necessary part of calculating an accurate price.

With details in hand, visit the website KBB. com or your local library for a hard copy of the latest book.

Get estimates for each of your cars and add them to your Asset list.

You can repeat this process for most other vehicles including boats, recreational vehicles, and motorcycles at NADAguides.com.

If you own an airplane, check these websites:

aircraftbluebook.com
naraaircraft.com

Chances are that if you are involved with planes, you either know the value already or you know people who can help you determine that figure.

After you've determined the value of your vehicles, add them to your Asset list.

Artwork, Furniture, Jewelry
If your fine jewelry or antique furniture is highly valuable you probably already have certain items insured outside your normal homeowners' policy.

Just be aware that insured or replacement value often does not equal resale value. In other words, you won't get nearly what they would be worth if sold in a retail environment.

More likely, you will sell the more valuable items essentially wholesale to a dealer or at a discounted price to the general public. If you're under time constraints, you will probably get less than if you could afford to wait and consign them with a dealer.

Seek out the appropriate dealers to get an idea of what the value might be and add that to your list if you plan to liquidate those items.

If your household goods such as furniture, rugs, and decorative accessories are of recent vintage and good quality you'll probably sell what you don't need at an estate or yard sale. An estate sales company can give you an estimate and handle all the details if you have a significant quantity of goods or if you prefer not to participate in the yard sale experience.

Likewise with most art. Few pieces are valuable enough to warrant a dealer or art auction's participation but you never know when a forgotten masterpiece might turn up.

If you have any doubts, contact the nearest professional for an evaluation. Estate liquidators have their own associations to help you locate members in your area. For more information visit the American Society of Estate Liquidators website:

aselonline.com

or the National Association of Estate Liquidators at:

estatesalesnews.com

Beware the expert who offers to buy your art or jewelry, however. That is usually a sure indication that your items will generate more interest and a higher price on the open market.

When you have a rough estimate of the total

value of these household items, add it to your list of Assets.

Animals and Hobby Equipment

Are you a collector or breeder of horses, llamas, exotic goats or endangered butterflies? If you're a serious owner or breeder, you likely know the value of your stock. If you're a casual owner of a few animals, you're probably more interested in re-homing them instead of outright selling them.

If appropriate, add these "unusuals" to your Asset list.

Maybe you have a hobby like organic gardening or a greenhouse filled with orchids. You may realize some money from selling plants and equipment. Or perhaps you have a small tractor or other specialized equipment.

These things can be hard to put a price to, and in some cases are more easily included in the sale of your home, either as value added or as available under separate contract.

One of the quickest ways to get a ballpark figure on these more exotic assets is to involve the aforementioned estate sales company or auction house. There are usually a few in any given area and a representative should be happy to visit your home and discuss the process with you. Of course, you will split the proceeds with the service provider.

As always, interview more than one if possible. You can also visit some estate sales as a secret shopper to evaluate different service providers.

Whichever way you decide to go, add a dollar amount for each category to your Asset list.

About letting go

Sorting through your possessions and deciding which ones you can live without is a difficult process for most of us. When a partner is involved, it can become even tougher to stay the course. You may have some heated discussions. Giving up the downsizing completely will begin to look like a very attractive alternative.

But the truth is, most of us own far more than we will ever need or use. You may have been accumulating stuff for many years – it's part of growing up and living as an adult. Realizing that part of your life is winding down can feel like an emotional wrecking ball crashing into your carefully constructed life.

Please know that this feeling is not unusual.

Approach the streamlining process with gratitude for the past and hope for the future. An attitude of appreciation for a well-lived life will help carry you through.

Remember, there is always professional assistance should you feel the need. Help ranges from organizers to relocation specialists to life transition coaches to counseling.

If you have children or friends who are interested in helping, get them involved, too.

Cash on hand

Under this category on your list, add the average amount you keep in checking and savings accounts.

Don't include investments or retirement accounts at this point, they come into play later on in the exercise.

We're not producing an official net worth figure, but the dollar amount you'll have to invest in a new home and lifestyle during the rightsizing process.

Liquid assets are addressed in the next chapter. In the meantime, here is a sample list of Assets.

ASSETS

Primary Residence: $_____

Vacation Home: $_____

Rental/Investment Property: $_____

Car: $_____

Boat: $_____

RV: $_____

Airplanes: $_____

Jewelry: $_____

Artwork: $_____

Furniture: $_____

Household Goods: $_____

Hobby Equipment/Animals: $_____

Cash on Hand: $_____

Worksheet

Available at sonyamyers.com/insiders

Net Worth

Assets		Liabilities	
Market Value of...		Outstanding Loan Balances on...	
Primary Residence:	_____	Primary Residence:	_____
Vacation Home:	_____	Vacation Home:	_____
Investment Property:	_____	Investment Property:	_____
Car:	_____	Line of credit:	_____
Car:	_____	Car:	_____
Boat:	_____	Car:	_____
RV:	_____	Boat:	_____
Airplane:	_____	RV:	_____
Jewelry:	_____	Airplane:	_____
Artwork:	_____	Other loans:	_____
Furniture:	_____	Credit card debt:	_____
Retirement Accounts:	_____	Credit card debt:	_____
Other Accounts/Misc:	_____	Credit card debt:	_____
Cash on Hand:	_____	Credit card debt:	_____
Total Assets:	$_____	**Total Liabilities:**	$_____

Calculate your net worth [Assets minus Liabilities]

Total Assets: $_____

Total Liabilities: $_____

Net Worth: $_____

Woohoo!

Chapter Five

What Are Your Liabilities?

The next step in calculating your net worth is figuring out how much you owe, or your Liabilities. The most convenient source for a ballpark figure is your monthly statements, either the paper or the online versions.

In either case, check your most recent statement for outstanding balances on the following:

- Mortgage
- Line of credit
- Auto loan
- Boat, RV, Airplane loans
- Student loans
- Credit cards

This activity will give you working numbers, which you can enter individually on your list under the heading of Liabilities. To get truly accurate numbers on the loans, you can call the various lenders and ask what your payoff would be as of a certain date in the near future, but that is not necessary at this point.

Things like utility bills, food, clothing allowance and dry cleaning bills don't belong on your list of liabilities. They are most likely charged to your credit cards or paid from your bank account, which we will address in the next step when we calculate your total net worth.

For now, simply add each item, until you have a complete list. For example:

LIABILITIES

Home loan: $_____

My car loan: $_____

Second car loan: $_____

RV loan: $_____

Credit card debt: $_____

When you have a complete list, it's time to bring out a calculator and complete the arithmetic.

Worksheet

Available at sonyamyers.com/insiders

Current Spending

Monthly Income

My Salary: _____

Spouse Salary: _____

Bonuses, etc.: _____

Bonuses, etc. _____

Investment Income, Stocks: _____

Investment Income, Rental Property: _____

Investment Income, Other: _____

Investment Income, Other: _____

Part-time Job: _____

Side Biz: _____

Other Income: _____

Total Income: $_____

Monthly Expenses

Mortgage: _____

Line of Credit: _____

Tax + Insurance: _____

Utilities: _____

Cable/Internet _____

Car Payments: _____

Auto Insurance: _____

Cell Phones: _____

Health Insurance: _____

Groceries/Toiletries: _____

Eating Out, etc.: _____

Credit Card Payments: _____

Other Expenses: _____

Total Expenses: $_____

Calculate your current bottom line

Total Monthly Income: $_____

Total Monthly Expenses: $_____

Total under or over: $_____

Happy or Sad?

DOWNSIZE YOUR HOME RIGHTSIZE YOUR LIFE WORKSHEETS © 2016 SONYAMYERS.COM

Chapter Six

Calculate Your Net Worth

Remember, your net worth is calculated by subtracting your total Liabilities from your total Assets.

Assets – Liabilities = Your Net Worth

Start a fresh sheet or add a page to your electronic document. At the top, write or type Net Worth.

Underneath that title, add the words Liquid Assets. Add up your total assets on the calculator and enter that number to the right of Liquid Assets.

Create a second line, labeled Retirement Accounts. Add up the current value of your investment and retirement accounts and enter that number to the right.

Now, you probably know the rough value of your investments and accounts. If you don't, you likely have so many that you should be reading a different book!

For the rest of us, the value of these accounts is a figure we are very well aware of.

What about the average person? According to the website Investopedia.com, a 2015 government study found 29% of Americans 55 and older don't have any retirement savings or pension. Of those who do, 55 to 64-year-olds have an average of $104,000 in savings.

Back to your numbers

Add up both of your Asset numbers and underline the figure.

Now, write down Liabilities. From the list you made earlier, add them up and enter the number to the right of Liabilities.

Next, write down Net Worth. Use a calculator to subtract your Liability number from your total Assets number. The result is your overall Net Worth. Underline that and circle it, decorating it with exclamation points and stars!

I hope the number impresses you. But even if it doesn't there is significant power in this number. Knowing is better than wondering and worrying.

Your sheet should look something like this:

NET WORTH
Liquid Assets $xxxxxx
Retirement Assets $xxxxxx
                    $<u>xxxxxx</u>

Subtract Liabilities $xxxxxx
Net Worth $XXXXXXX

The simple formula

To restate the overriding goal here: tap the equity in your home, buy a less expensive home, and use the extra cash to help finance your retirement.

In an ideal world, you won't have to draw on your investments or retirement accounts to do that, so work with the numbers in your Liquid Assets list only. These are actual physical items you can convert to cash, and are the ones listed on the downloadable worksheets.

It is my hope that you can move forward without selling your cars, boat, and other vehicles. But if you must rightsize those in service of your ultimate lifestyle, you must.

For now, take the estimated market value of your home and subtract the outstanding mortgage or line of credit if you have one.

This figure is your working budget. Write it in big letters at the bottom of your Net Worth sheet. In fact, write it on a slip of paper for your wallet. Write it in your journal and on your bathroom mirror. Keep that number firmly in your mind as we continue to work through your retirement budget.

Worksheet

Available at sonyamyers.com/insiders

Future Spending

Monthly Income

Social Security/Pension: _____

Spouse SS/Pension: _____

Investment Income, Stocks: _____

Investment Income, Rental Property: _____

Investment Income, 401(k), etc. _____

Investment Income, IRA, etc. _____

Part-time Job: _____

Side Biz: _____

Other Income: _____

Total Income: $_____

Monthly Expenses

Property Taxes _____

Homeowners Insurance: _____

Utilities: _____

Cable/Internet _____

Car Payments, Maintenance: _____

Auto Insurance: _____

Cell Phones: _____

Health Insurance: _____

Groceries/Toiletries: _____

Eating Out, etc.: _____

Other Expenses: _____

Total Expenses: $_____

Calculate your future bottom line

Total Monthly Income: $_____

Total Monthly Expenses: $_____

Total under or over: $_____

Better Now?

DOWNSIZE YOUR HOME RIGHTSIZE YOUR LIFE WORKSHEETS © 2016 SONYAMYERS.COM

Chapter Seven

Your Retirement Budget

Start working on a retirement budget to get an idea of how different scenarios will work for your situation.

We talk about the big picture here with expense and income categories being fairly broad. That's a good place to start, although you can get a lot more detailed once you've made some of the bigger decisions.

Following are the basic categories of income and expenses. Grab a notebook and jot down the relevant categories then plug in your numbers.

You can use the worksheet from my site or you can get more formal with an actual spreadsheet if you prefer. The more complex your finances, the more likely you'll need a spreadsheet.

INCOME

Your Social Security

Spouse Social Security

Your pension

Spouse pension

Investment income

Savings withdrawal

      Total monthly income

EXPENSES

Property Tax & Insurance

Utilities

Groceries & toiletries

Cable/Internet

Car payments

Car insurance

Health insurance

Other insurance

Credit card payments

      Total monthly expenses

We're looking for a rough working number at this point, and assuming you will have no mortgage or rent. If you do, simply add that category.

About SSN

Your Social Security payment is figured using a complex calculation based on a 35-year average of your covered wages. Each year's wages are adjusted for inflation before being averaged.

If you worked longer than 35 years, the government will use the highest 35 years. If you worked fewer than 35 years, they average in zeros for the years you are lacking. If you can avoid zeros by working a couple of years longer, you'll increase your Social Security payment.

If you don't know when you're eligible to claim benefits, consult the information available at:

SSA.gov

Once you know your earliest possible date, consider the two schools of thought on when to claim your Social Security benefits. The first option, promoted by most financial planners, is to wait as long as possible so you'll receive the highest amount available.

The second option is to sign up as soon as you are eligible. Either way, you are basically gambling on how long you will live.

For example, if your full retirement age is 66 and you decide to retire early at 62, your benefits will be reduced by 25%. If you waited until 66, and would receive $1,000 per month at that time, retiring at 62 will result in $750 per month instead.

Sure, you'll get more per month the longer you wait. But what impact will working those extra years have? Might your lifespan be shortened? Might your health worsen due to stress? What experiences will you have missed in the meantime?

These are questions only you can answer. Just keep in mind that by claiming early, you'll receive benefits longer.

On the other hand, if you claim at 62, you'll still pay your own health insurance until age 65, when Medicare kicks in. Complicated, isn't it?

Retired law professor and Social Security expert Merton Bernstein believes the longevity odds are bad, so claim early. "You never know when the bell will ring. I subscribe to the Woody

Allen principal: "Take the money and run.'"

You can find a wealth of additional information at MyRetirementPaycheck.org, a website sponsored by the National Endowment for Financial Education.

Case Study

For an imaginary family of two adults with no pets, consider the following scenario.

Dan and Carol, both age 64, netted $400,000 on the sale of their family home (after closing costs and paying off a small home equity line of credit). They bought a smaller single family home for $200,000 and put the remainder in a savings account. They downsized to a single car and both plan to participate in Medicare Part B at age 65.

Assuming a 20-year retirement time line and good health, here is their budget.

INCOME

Dan's Social Security	$1,100
Carol's pension	$1,100
200K Savings withdrawal	$800
Total monthly income	$3,000

EXPENSES

Property Tax & Insurance	$275
Utilities	$90
Groceries	$440
Cable/Internet	$50
Car insurance	$75
Health insurance (Medicare B)	$240
Total monthly expenses	$1,170

Subtracting Expenses from Income, on paper Dan and Carol's monthly surplus is $1,830.

$3,000 - $1,170 = $1,830

Of course, there are many more possible expenses but these are the essentials for most of us. The surplus is available for hobbies, travel, eating out, entertaining, or setting aside for the inevitable expenses of maintaining a single-family home.

Your Worksheet

Create and fill out your preliminary worksheet to get your own income and expense numbers.

Recognize the property tax and insurance amount is the most flexible item on the list. That figure will depend on how much house you buy, as well as where you buy it, due to differences in property tax rates in different areas.

Once you have a handle on your available funds, you can consider several ways to downsize your housing needs.

One more factor to consider is your capacity for downsizing. How far are you willing to go? Fortunately "things" matter less as we age, but the entire process can be fraught with grief and loss.

For most of us, letting go of a cherished home and valued possessions can equal the loss of associated memories. That is painful, no matter how you look at it. The key is to anticipate the struggle, know how to get support, and keep the end result in mind.

If you need more help than your friends and family network can provide, find a certified coach who specializes in retirement issues to help you deal with the discomfort.

Where to retire
Perhaps you plan to stay in your current area, close to friends and family. You know the real estate market and have a good idea of what your

money will buy.

But if you plan to relocate to a retirement destination or favorite vacation destination the financial picture can change dramatically.

Say your housing budget for a cash purchase is $200,000. You might buy a lovely small single family home or villa for $200,000 in many parts of the country but if you dream of living on the beach, that same $200,000 might only buy an 800 square foot condo with monthly fees in the $400-800 range.

Where you retire can have an immense impact on your quality of life, both positive and negative. Choosing the right place is critical to your success and long term happiness.

As with most situations, being prepared and knowing what to expect can lower your stress levels.

Chapter Eight

Find Your Town

Working with a lot of buyers and sellers as an agent, I see one mistake the newly retired make over and over again. That is falling in love with a house before considering the community and big picture.

Here's a personal example. When we first started looking a number of years back, we visited the Hill Country of Texas near Austin. We wandered around for days, soaking up the atmosphere and meeting the locals.

In one charming town we visited an open house. The property was located high on a hillside with a dramatic view. It was a thoroughly charming farmhouse with a picket fence and extensive outdoor space in a pleasant neighborhood with meandering streets shaded by ancient oak trees. I loved it.

My practical minded husband looked closely at the property taxes. If you are familiar with Texas you already know this. Property taxes in that state are spectacularly high, in fact in 2016 Texas had the fourth highest property tax rate in the nation.

That was a rude awakening. We had to relegate Texas to the "nice place to visit, but don't want to buy there" category.

But it's a big country. How will you ever decide on where to retire? Start with the process of elimination. If you have already decided to retire to another home in your current area, just skip this chapter and go on to the next.

But if you are still considering where to live next, read on. There are many lists of best places to retire, most economical towns, and so forth. It seems like a new list comes out every week. That's how we ended up in the Hill Country, by the way.

Having followed these lists for years and visited many of the towns profiled I can tell you one thing without a doubt: there is no substitute for spending some time in an area. Do not decide it sounds good on paper and then pick up and move there.

That's another mistake my husband and I made, in 2006. It was a long hot summer in Fayetteville, Arkansas and the property next door had just been sold to a developer. Our lovely view of fenced pastures and Arabian horses was about to be subdivided and scraped raw for eventual erection of the dreaded McMansions so popular back then.

I had started having hot flashes and suggested we take an exploratory road trip to the Oregon coast. So we packed up the RV and headed west. Oregon was chilly, rugged and vastly different. We spend two weeks there before returning home.

Later, thinking even further north would be better, we flew to Whidbey Island north of Seattle and vacationed in a cottage for about a week. Google revealed the area didn't experience as much rain as Seattle and it was an island, two very desirable traits in our book at the time.

Naturally, we returned home and proceeded to sell our property. Sight unseen, we rented a furnished house in Sequim, just across the Strait of Juan de Fuca from Whidbey. We had our furniture loaded onto a moving van, packed up two cats and headed out.

It took us a couple of months to find our jumbo-sized three story faux-Victorian house in Coupeville. We moved in and lasted about six months. Nowhere did Google mention the constant cold, damp wind the upper San Juan islands enjoy during the winter months. Basically, it blows straight across the ocean from Japan right into Whidbey Island.

Our bones hurt. Our eyes dried out. We walked to the nearby post office bundled up in layers of polar fleece and never really got warm that winter.

One day I'd had it. My husband sent me a MLS link to a house on a hillside in Fayetteville, and three days later I boarded a plane to go look at it. A few weeks after that we were packing the moving van to head back south.

The icing on the cake? The country was teetering on the edge of the real estate bubble and it took us years to sell that Whidbey Island house.

The moral of that story is try it before you buy it! Spend enough time in your dream location to see if you can tolerate the worst of its weather before you invest your money in buying a house. Rent instead.

While you may be loathe to part with your hard-earned retirement dollars, exploring potential destinations is money well spent.

Imagine your retirement cache as a huge pile of money. Because it is. How much physical space would $500,000 – for example – take up if you piled it on your floor? Maybe a stack three feet high?

Then imagine the paltry thousands you might spend if you stay at a hotel or short term rental in your dream location. Compared to the big pile, it will likely be a little tiny stack less than an inch tall.

Think of rent in those terms, money well spent if it saves you from an expensive mistake like the one we made.

Here is another resource for advance research on possible locations: City-Data.com, a website that collects and analyzes information to create detailed profiles of "all cities" in the country. The site also has forums where you can ask specific questions that are answered by area residents.

Just be aware that many of those who answer are real estate agents, as City Data is a major source of leads. Still, there is a ton of info on various topics and the site is well worth your time and attention as you build a list of possible retirement locations.

Once you have locations, you can spend time visiting and eliminating those that won't work for you in one way or another.

Once you've found your town, you can get serious about selling the old house.

Chapter Nine
Sell Your House & Stuff

This might be a good time to remind you that downsizing is not necessarily the answer for everyone. Your family traditions, size, and overall way of life might not benefit from the process. After considering the facts, you may decide that you're just the right size already. And that's okay.

But if you have decided to take the plunge, the first order of business is converting your real estate and excess worldly possessions into cash.

In the previous chapter on Assets, I discussed how to get a market analysis from a Realtor. I hope you found the agent you want to hire during that process.

To reinforce the conversation you likely had

with your agent about de-cluttering and curb appeal, here is my best advice on getting your house ready to put on the market. It's based on over 20 years spent buying, renovating and then selling 12 different houses in eight different towns. That's 24 transactions, not including the friends and associates I helped before I even got a real estate license myself. This is the same advice I give to sellers I work with.

1. Plan to take an extended trip right before the listing goes live on your local Multiple Listing Service (MLS) if you possibly can. Make sure you're available via phone and internet connection, so your agent can communicate offers, though.

The process will be a lot less traumatic if you're not in residence for the constant state of extreme neatness and short notice showings required to get top dollar for your house in the shortest amount of time.

I realize this may not be a practical option for some, but consider getting away for as long as you can, even if you visit friends or relatives. It solves a lot of potential problems like requiring agents to set advance appointments, racing around to tidy up and secure your valuables at a moment's notice, and finding ways to spend your time while barred from your home during showings.

And yes, you absolutely must leave your home during showings. Few things make a potential buyer more uncomfortable than having the homeowner lingering about. Buyers must be able to envision themselves living in your space. That's hard to pull off when you're sitting there on your sofa watching TV or pretending to read a book while you eavesdrop on the buyer/agent conversation. It's extremely awkward and a waste of time for all involved.

But if you can leave for the first few weeks after listing, you will avoid the worst of the inconvenience. Of course, you'll want some security measures in place or possibly a home watch service. At the very least, your agent should stop by after a showing to make sure everything is locked up and the lights turned off.

2. Pack up your favorite possessions and put them in storage. Rent air conditioned or heated storage space, as the extra money is worth it to preserve the condition of your prized furniture, extra clothing, artwork, etc.

By the way, if you are attached to a particular

painting or light fixture, replace it with one from a big box store before your agent takes photos for the listing.

Why? Many times a buyer will fall in love with one thing in your house and insist on hinging the entire deal on it. This happens with paintings, furniture, and even pets.

When we sold our rural blueberry farm in the mountains of northwest Arkansas, the Denver buyers asked for our two cats to be included in the sale. We agreed, because what they didn't know was that we had agonized over whether to relocate those barn-raised, free range rat slayers from their 40-acre kingdom into a suburban neighborhood where they would have to live indoors to survive.

While pets don't often come into the equation, you may have a favorite piece of art, furniture, or decorative item like a chandelier that you're loathe to part with. If it's locked away in storage, a buyer can't make an offer contingent on including it.

3. Pack up or dispose of all but the essentials, including excess bookcases and other unnecessary furniture. The house will look more spacious. Stage the entire house including the garage to look like a model home, not like you actually live there. Organize everything left in the closets and cupboards so the place looks like a shelter magazine photo spread.

Out goes anything you don't use on a very frequent basis. Consider this advance downsizing as you throw away old cosmetics, worn out clothing, and stacks of magazines. Start a collection of samples, unused products and seldom worn clothing for the local thrift store or nursing home.

For those sentimental items that are hard to let go, "Take a photo of the item before you donate it. Print the photos and journal every detail of the experience you had with the item," says Anna Newell Jones, author of *The Spender's Guide to Debt-Free Living*. "Write it all out, either on actual paper or on your computer. Write out in stunning detail every single itty bitty detail you can remember."

Start as early as possible, so you'll have time to carefully consider what stays and what goes. Believe me, if you wait until you're packing up the entire house to move one of two things will happen: you'll move a bunch of unnecessary crap with you or you will fill many garbage bags with stuff you suddenly realize you haven't used in ages and don't really need after all. Those bags will go straight into the trash.

4. Hire a professional house cleaning service. Even if you keep a spotless home, the pros will fine-tune and improve on your work. Especially if your house needs updating, extreme cleanliness will impress buyers.

It will also put you one step ahead when it comes to the home inspection. The inspector might pull out the stove or refrigerator during inspection. Have you any idea what might be back there? Imagine dribbles of spaghetti sauce down the side of an adjacent cabinet. Tiny piles of unidentifiable brown stuff. Petrified dust bunnies? One look at whatever is growing down there could put your buyers off the deal.

Buyers are demanding these days. It's the HGTV effect: real estate shoppers expect perfection. They are finicky and subconsciously looking for an excuse to get out of the deal. Eliminate as many objections as possible – don't let years' worth of cooking oil splatters, crumbs and mystery fluff alienate a potential buyer.

5. Store or disguise equipment or medicines suggesting poor health. Likewise personal hygiene products, bug spray, lawn chemicals, etc.

Basically, buyers don't like to be reminded that actual people live in "their" dream home. They are turned off by anything associated with normal day to day functions. Damp washcloths, toilet seats left in the upright position, dirty clothes or dishes, leftovers in the fridge, oil spots on the driveway; the list is endless.

Just think of what you would find gross in a stranger's home and get rid of it in yours. Or store such items in decorative baskets, boxes or other containers.

I once disguised a grungy, random rock collection in a set of white plastic buckets on a garage shelf, which looked neat, tidy, and innocuous. Storage doesn't have to be expensive, and consistency goes a long way toward reinforcing the concept of a neat and orderly home.

See why I say it's best to just leave for a while? Buyers want to imagine themselves in your space leading a fantasy life that doesn't include mundane activities like cleaning house or suffering from a severe bout of flu.

In addition, anything less than a squeaky clean and super tidy presentation to potential buyers results in an attempt to bargain down your price, if they bother to make an offer at all.

Assuming you price your house to sell, taking these steps will position you for maximum gain. Your agent will surely have additional information to share, as real estate is local in nature. Customs and expectations may differ in your area. At a minimum, expect to declutter, paint or touch up the paint inside and out, freshen the landscaping, power wash the driveway, and remove heavy window coverings.

Selling your stuff

Take the same approach to selling your other possessions: super clean, tidy, and priced to sell at the best price the market will bear.

A note about furniture, household liquidations and estate sales: things don't usually bring as much as you think they should at these events. Nowhere near what you paid for them, in most cases.

With so Baby Boomers retiring and downsizing, there are a lot of estate sales taking place. The generations behind us don't value the same things we do and in fact are trending toward the "less is more" philosophy that many of us are just now beginning to embrace.

For example, a living room set that you paid $3,000 for might be worth a few hundred dollars if it's in excellent condition. Plenty of pre-owned furniture is available at garage sales and thrift stores. In many parts of the country, resale stores are awash in used furniture.

In my area, Goodwill and Salvation Army are quite selective about what they will accept due to the huge volume of household liquidations and post-moving sales held by those going through the retiring and downsizing process.

According to Julie Hall, of the American Society of Estate Liquidators, the average estate sales proceeds are $7,000-$15,000. And the sales agency commission can vary, impacting the bottom line significantly.

If you decide to hire an estate sales company, do your research to make sure their reputation is good. Check their association memberships and online reviews, at a minimum. Do they carry adequate insurance or are you liable if someone claims injury during the sale? Does your homeowners insurance include liability coverage?

If you prefer to go it alone with a sale, here are a few tips on best practices, safety, and security. Not familiar with this type of event? Do a bit of research online or visit a few local sales. They can get very hectic, so preparation is key.

Yard sale tips

In general, keep the big picture in mind. If you worry that you're too close to your things to be objective, ask a friend or family member to help you. Here are a few other helpful hints:

- **Recruit helpers.** The larger the sale, the more assistance you'll need to keep track of who wants what, negotiate prices, and collect money.

- **Play some background tunes.** Give your event a little style with your musical selections. Nothing too loud or trendy, just a little mood music.

- **Price to sell.** Forget what you paid or what an item is worth. You're downsizing, remember? As your sale winds down, lower your prices. You might even offer a "clear this table" deal to a single person who will take a lot of things for one low price. Because you really don't want to haul all that stuff back into your house, or have to deal with donating it or throwing it away.

- **Secure pets and valuables**. In the whirlwind environment of a sale, dogs and cats get overstimulated. Consider restricting them to one room for their own safety or take them to a friend's house for the duration.

- **Lock up medicine, jewelry, and valuables** or remove them from the premises. People tend to wander at these events and crimes of opportunity can take place.

- **Block off access to private areas.** Lock doors or at the very least, put up signs that indicate which areas are off limits. Lock your bedroom door if possible. Ideally, your sale will take place in the garage or outside. Set up your payment table blocking the door to the inside and refuse access to anyone who asks.

- **Beware large groups of shoppers** who attempt to roam around toward the back of your home, as well as anyone who insists her child needs your bathroom. It's not uncommon for unscrupulous types to case future targets by attending garage sales. Be ready to deny access or refer people to the nearest public facilities.

- **Wear a fanny pack** to keep cash on your person. Even smaller sales can generate a lot of dollar bills and loose change. Leaving money accessible on a table or in a box puts it at risk.

Community sale sites

If you're listing items on a site like Craigslist, take proper precautions. Always have someone with you when allowing a stranger into your home. Accept cash only and beware large bills.

Don't fall for the scammer's trick of accepting a wire transfer in excess of the amount you're asking. The scammer will ask you to send the balance of the overpayment back. Then their original payment funds are fraudulent, in which case you're out all that money and the property you sold, as well.

In some cases, it might be easier to call Habitat For Humanity or another local group to donate your unwanted household goods and take the tax write-offs available for charitable donations. How quickly do you want to move on and what is your tolerance for this sort of detail? Only you can decide.

Habitat For Humanity is a nonprofit organization that builds affordable housing in partnership with volunteers, sponsors and corporate donors. Habitat operates ReStore centers where you can donate all kinds of unwanted items, from old windows and appliances to excess inventory. Donated items are sold to support their mission locally.

Chapter Ten

Find The Right New Home

There are several rightsize options for housing, including the single-family home, the villa, the condo, and the manufactured home.

Generally speaking, that's a rough order of cost, until you factor in location. Take Florida for example. A single-family home a few miles from the coast might cost as little as $150,000 - $200,000 depending on its size and age. The exact same home would cost two to three times as much if located within a few blocks of the beach or on boating water.

Once you have found your town or community, focus on your budget to determine what type of home in your desired location fits into your plan.

Remember, if you sell a $600,000 home

and buy a $200,000 single family home, you are effectively cutting your overhead by two-thirds (unless you're so close to the coast that insurance costs are higher than normal).

But if you decide to spend that $200,000 on a villa or condo or a manufactured/mobile home, there are other expenses to consider. Homeowner Association (HOA) fees and maintenance are the two most common ones.

Maybe you like the idea of the lock-it-and-leave option provided by a condominium. In addition to the utilities, you'll have HOA fees that go toward exterior maintenance and insurance. The closer to the coast, the higher insurance and building maintenance costs are, therefore the higher your mandatory HOA fees will be.

Villas fit in between single family homes and condos as far as costs go, with the location and age again figuring into the equation.

Another option to dramatically decrease your overall housing cost is the manufactured home.

Here's a case in point. In the beach community where I live there are two homes, each of which last sold in 1999 so the property taxes are largely based on that year's sales price for each one.

The stick-built or "bricks and mortar" single family home sold for $269,900 and the property tax in 2015 was $2,963 (two thousand nine hundred sixty-three dollars).

A nearby manufactured home in a co-op community of a similar neighborhood sold for $158,000 and the property tax in 2015 was $577 (five hundred seventy-seven dollars). I will get to why in just a second.

Property taxes for the single-family home were five times as high as the manufactured home.

If you had bought the manufactured home – in addition to the investment savings of $111,900 – you would have put an extra $198 tax savings in your bank account each month.

In ten years, that totals $23,860 saved on property taxes alone. Plus, the initial savings on the purchase price of $111,900 equals $135,760.

Divide that by 10 years and you would gain $13,576 each year for investing or travel or additional leisure activities or what have you.

Granted, there are other expenses to consider, like insurance, monthly fees to cover recreational facilities and lawn care, etc. And the difference in maintenance and repairs to the house versus the mobile home, or manufactured home.

Now before you protest that you will never live in one of those tacky trailer parks, consider the following.

Paradise Cove in Malibu, California is famous not only for its coastal location, but also for its well-known residents like Matthew McConaughey, Pamela Anderson, and Minnie Driver. Homes in the Cove sell between $250,000 and $2.5 million. Like many parks, residents don't own the land. They pay monthly lot rents of up to $1,850, but don't pay property taxes.

My friend Jean's sister recently spent in the neighborhood of half a million dollars for a mobile home on the shore in New Jersey. It's her vacation home now, and perhaps her retirement home in the future. (According to the Manufactured Housing Institute, 23% of manufactured home owners are retired.)

So manufactured homes, or "house trailers" are not necessarily the housing option of last resort some people might envision. The economics of trailer life can allow you to indulge in an otherwise relatively extravagant lifestyle.

That's the beauty of this process. There's room for many different lifestyles. Each situation will require some very personalized math, and the overall scenario will vary. It almost requires a spreadsheet to effectively evaluate the overall cost and savings. You can create a paper version on a legal pad, as the number of overall options makes creating a digital one a bit cumbersome.

No matter what you decide, stay organized by using the Community Worksheet you'll create in the Resources section at the end of this book or with my downloadable version.

Another way to stay organized is to start a file on potential towns and communities. Print pages from their websites and highlight details for those that meet your criteria. Or if you're techy, keep track online with an app like Evernote.

Deed Restrictions

One very important chunk of information is the community deed restrictions or restrictive covenants.

These are exactly like they sound; rules and

regulations that pertain to the use of the land and look of the neighborhood. Essentially, deed restrictions limit your control of your own property, in a good way.

Typically, either the HOA or the home's listing agent will prepare a list of frequently asked questions (FAQs) that cover the most common restrictions and required fees. This information might also be provided in the form of a Seller's Disclosure.

If the preliminary information passes muster, request the complete deed restriction document and read it carefully.

This step is critical, because you don't want to invest your money in a home where the neighborhood rules make life difficult.

If you're not willing to abide by certain rules, move on. It's that simple. There is plenty of real estate for sale. You want to surround yourself with people who share your values and lifestyle so that retirement will be as fulfilling as possible.

As you review these options, start to think about how you spend your money now and how you will spend it in your retirement. (It may help to keep a spending log for a month to really dig deep into where your money goes.)

Then look at the various properties for sale in your target area and start calculating how much you could save if you traded your current home for one of these options.

And think of all you could do and experience, what a different life you could lead, with your overhead reduced as you move forward.

If you've been building a list from magazines or online research, the next step is to visit your top picks and find a Realtor to assist in your home search. Again, interview three agents. Pick one in the mid-range, with enough time to devote to your exploratory search and enough experience to do a good job negotiating the best possible terms when you are ready to buy.

A few words about the relationship with your chosen agent. First, be honest about where you are in the process. If you're evaluating the community, it doesn't make sense to involve an agent and schedule showings at this point.

If you want to know how much house you can get for your money, do your research with model homes, real estate magazines and open houses in addition to the internet. Don't waste an agent's time when you just want to tour the area.

When you are ready to seriously shop for a property, by all means pick an agent and stay with her. Please don't "agent hop" or use more than one agent in a geographic area. It's confusing and potentially a problem down the line.

When you want to make an offer, which agent writes it and handles the negotiation? The one you contacted on the internet who sent you a bunch of listings, or the one you met at the coffee shop who made appointments and accompanied you on showings? You can see how it gets confusing.

Remember, all active agents have access to the same properties on the MLS. If one claims she has a special relationship with a particular new home builder or a number of "pocket listings" not on the open market, walk the other way.

When you are ready to get serious, here is one step to take that will give you an edge, which you might need if your target area is one experiencing a hot real estate market.

Before you go

Before you leave home, print out what is known as "proof of funds." This information, which you can share with your agent, will demonstrate that you are serious and have the means to buy.

Some experienced agents require either proof of funds or a mortgage lender's letter of pre-approval before showing property. Don't be offended, it's a common practice. Just be sure to black out your account numbers and address on statements, leaving only your name and account balance visible. In fact, you can simply show it to the agent if you're not comfortable providing an actual copy to her.

Another option, if you have a close relationship with a smaller bank, is to get a signed letter stating you have X amount of funds available in your accounts. And don't be surprised if the agent calls to confirm the letter is legitimate. It's business.

Your agent is a valuable resource who can guide you through the process. If you haven't bought property lately, share that with the agent and ask all the questions you need to feel comfortable with the process.

Here is what *not* to do: go into a hot seller's market and insist on making offers that are way below asking price. Your agent will share recent statistics on what is called the List-to-Sale ratio, which is an average of the asking price compared to the actual sales price of comparable properties.

In my area right now, 96% is not uncommon. So a home listed for $200,000 would sell for $192,000 on the average. The range for similar homes might be from 94% to 100% or full price, but the average is usually a good indicator of where you will end up.

Can you see how it wouldn't make sense to offer the seller $150,000 or even $175,000? It would be a waste of your time and the agent's time, as the seller would probably decline to enter negotiations with an unrealistic or "low-balling" buyer. Of course, there is a lot more to say about the negotiation process, but this book is about downsizing, not sales strategy.

Keep in mind that in addition to local knowledge and connections you might appreciate in the future, your agent is the gateway to an entire community of service providers. If you act like the mature, professional adult you are during the process, you can gain access to these handymen, plumbers, painters, etc.

If you let stress get the best of you and have a meltdown, you might find yourself on your own in locating service providers and getting advice in the future. In a successful relationship, you and your agent will stay in touch, with you asking for her recommendations from time to time and sending your friends to her as well, if they are interested in buying property in your new area.

If the experience is less than cordial on either side, don't fret. There is a real estate agent on practically every corner in many popular retirement destinations. For example, official figures indicate that one in every 175 Florida residents was a Realtor in 2012. And that was before the market really heated up and many new or returning agents joined the field; the National Association of Realtors estimates that 167,771 agents have joined the association in the past three years.

In 2012, Florida was surpassed only by Arizona where one in every 168 residents was a Realtor and Hawaii where one in every 173 residents was a Realtor.

Compare that to Idaho for example, where only one in 267 residents was a Realtor. When you consider the population and that Realtors are concentrated mostly in destination markets, you won't be surprised when almost everybody you meet in a Florida beach community or Arizona retirement town is either an agent or knows one they can recommend to you.

Do yourself a favor and don't commit to an agent until you have met him or her in person. Online relationships are not the same as real ones and sometimes those who recommend an agent are technically "referral agent" license holders who get paid a portion of the commission if you buy a home.

Instead, walk into a few real estate offices or pick up a magazine and call around to find several agents to interview before you decide which one will help you make this momentous decision. Or visit open houses to meet agents and observe their style and personality.

By the way, the primary difference between a Realtor and a real estate agent is this: A real estate agent is anyone who is licensed to help people buy and sell property. Realtor is a trademarked term that refers to an agent who is licensed and also an active member of the National Association of Realtors (NAR), and who upholds certain standards and abides by a code of ethics.

Alternatives to buying

You can, of course, rent living space while you take the time to adjust and consider your options. Many of the same overhead concepts apply and it's easy to do the math.

One benefit of renting is that the landlord assumes the cost of property taxes and some types of insurance.

One drawback is that in popular retirement destinations, there is a lot of competition for rental properties. The rental rates also tend to be higher. Often it is easier to buy a place than rent one!

Another option is living in a recreational vehicle (RV). This is a huge trend among Boomers. While it's hard to say how many enjoy this living arrangement as the definition of full time is rather fluid, suffice it to say, "A lot!" Estimates range between 250,000 to a million people who claim an RV as their permanent residence.

RV prices range from the occasional low cost fixer-upper to the hundreds of thousands for a high-end model. In addition to the cost of the actual RV and ongoing maintenance, consider how much you'll pay for gas to travel from one area to another and the fees you'll pay for lot rental at your destination. It's a fascinating lifestyle. A number of books have been written on the subject, as well as numerous blogs by active full-timers.

In many ways, finding your new home is the easiest part of this process. You will already have the money, you will have done the research and you will know how to get the assistance you need from an agent.

Now it's almost time to put it all together, working toward the vision you created as you designed your new life. You have a financial plan, a few ideas about where to retire, and the information you need to begin the rigorous process of downsizing.

But first, consider some of the pitfalls you may face along the way.

Chapter Eleven

Potential Problems

There are a few situations and people who can stand in the way of your retirement goals. Among these are poor health or a sudden health emergency, family members who feel entitled to oppose your plans, and your own indecision. Not to mention increasingly sophisticated scammers, out to separate you from your money.

Your health

A recent study by Fidelity Investments estimates that today's 65-year-old can expect to spend an average of $130,000 on health care in retirement for just premiums, co-payments, and non-covered items like eyeglasses. Divide that by the life expectancy of 20 years are you're talking $6,500 a year — if nothing goes wrong with your health. The answer of course is to beat the average by staying in tip top health.

A health emergency is another possibility. These tend to happen suddenly and can require a significant amount of money to address. Make sure you have access to cash in the amount of your plan's deductibles and out of pocket expense limits so the financial stress will be minimized and you can focus on healing.

Lack of community

We are hard-wired for connection, even the most introverted among us. Just as the body feels pain as a result of real hunger, the mind feels pain as a result of loneliness. Loneliness results in negativity, and the cycle continues.

So we stay home in our big expensive houses, avoid physical activity and people, and eat processed food. The more we indulge in this type of activity, the more seductive and ingrained it becomes. Does that sound like a recipe for personal disaster or what?

The kids and other family members

Another potential roadblock to rightsizing is your family. Now maybe you love to support your children by acting as free babysitter, chauffeur, and occasional piggy bank. Maybe you want to move in with the kids so you can cook, clean and transport the grandchildren while your son or daughter goes back to work.

Perhaps fulfilling this role is your pleasure. Or perhaps you are slipping into the position by default or lack of a better plan.

Another potential landmine: You may be surprised to learn that your own spouse has a different idea of retirement than you do. I will never forget the look of shock and dismay on the face of my friend Claire when her husband revealed his assumption that they would travel the world on a cruise ship in retirement, when all she wanted to do was move to the New England coast and paint seascapes.

No doubt they had many interesting discussions later, and happily they eventually compromised on shorter cruises and a small condo on the coast.

In either case, take a hard look at your future. How do you want to live it? Is your spouse in agreement with your vision?

If so, that's wonderful for all involved. But if you have another path in mind, you must summon your strength for some difficult conversations where you stand up for your own desires, rather than capitulate to someone else's idea of the right life for you.

The financial advisers

Surprisingly, resistance may come from your own investment team, or your accountant. Both may be heavily "invested" in maintaining the status quo and their own cash flow position.

Whether it's the conservative CPA or the heavy trading stock broker, don't just assume these professionals put your desires and best interests ahead of their own. Like some successful real estate agents, they may be more interested in their own bottom lines than your happiness.

I don't mean to insult or malign your trusted service providers. I *do* want you to be prepared in case you meet resistance from these quarters. Going through the rightsize process mentally and on paper will help you clarify your plans and help you maintain your resolve once your plans are in place.

Your own social circle

Retirement is one of those life events that separate the wheat from the chaff. It's kind of like divorce or financial ruin that way, when you learn who your real friends are.

If your friends disapprove after you have an honest conversation about your plans, just mourn the loss and move on. You'll make new friends and at some point in the future those naysayers may come to understand when they face the same lifestyle and financial decisions as you are wrestling with right now.

Indecision, isolation, depression

Face it, the many details involved and choices you have to make as retirement approaches can be overwhelming. It is so much easier to do nothing or to take the advice of your friends and family and just hang in there while they decide what is best for you.

The sheer amount of work it takes to pull together the information and organize your thoughts is mind-boggling. Not to mention the cascading series of decisions required to navigate the process of downsizing.

Yes, there may be days when it seems impossible. When you change your mind several times and start to feel put upon and isolated, incapable of making one more choice. Maybe even a bit depressed.

This is to be expected. Any major life change, even a positive one, can spark depression. It's tied into loss and grieving. There are many losses involved in this process, big and small. Literally each thing you toss, give away or sell is a loss. Many items represent memories so it can feel like you are losing those treasured feelings, too.

But memories don't live in things, memories live in your heart and your soul. Things serve to remind us of the memories, that's all.

That said, keep something if the memory it invokes is priceless and you feel it will be lost to you without the item. Hopefully it will be a small something like a pearl necklace, not a big something like an armoire or a vintage automobile.

It helps to have an antidote on standby. I'm not talking about vodka here, but touching base with a close friend who supports you or taking an energizing walk around the block when you're feeling overwhelmed. A pleasant distraction can be enough to break the bottleneck of emotion and let your feelings flow and eventually even out.

And feel the emotion you must, because

ignoring it will only compound the problem. Overwhelm is a part of the process. Perhaps it is your system telling you to take a break. What's the hurry anyway? You're about to be retired, when you'll have all the time in the world!

Scammers

Speaking of all the time in the world, you'll also have plenty of time to answer your phone or check your email. Both are prime avenues of access for scammers.

It seems there is a new tactic each week. A grandchild calls with a money emergency. You won the sweepstakes and need only pay a funds transfer fee. The IRS says you owe back taxes and you are about to be arrested if you don't immediately provide a credit card for payment. The utilities will be cut off, etc.

This is the flip side of a problem we discussed in how to sell your stuff, where a scammer will send you an overpayment if you will only refund the difference.

Here, the scammer bullies or threatens you into paying money you don't owe. The explanations can be very convincing. The caller knows your grandchild's name and where he went on spring break. Or what utility company provides your electricity.

Don't buy it. If someone you don't know calls you on the phone feel free to hang up without engaging in conversation. Many of us were raised to be polite. We respect the ring of a phone and the chime of a doorbell and feel it would be rude to ignore them.

However, times have changed. This is a new world, and you are in control of it. Well, as much as we can be in control of anything, to be realistic.

If you don't want to answer the phone let it go to voice mail. Or if your primary phone is a cell, increasingly popular these days, install an app like Mr. Number that identifies suspected spam numbers. And as a public service, report those calls you get that you suspect are scams. It's easy to do on most apps, just Google it for the one you use.

About that knock on the door or ring of the bell. Feel free to just ignore it. Or look out a window and then decide whether you will answer. Worried about feeling embarrassed or silly? Summon your cranky old lady and enjoy the feeling of control when you make the decisions over what you will and will not do. Just go about your preferred business. It's empowering.

The costly renovation

If you buy a resale instead of a new home, chances are it will need some work. Maybe a lot of work, and at a higher cost than is budget friendly.

Whether you choose to buy a home that needs a little or a lot of work, proceed with caution. Consider, is this how you want to spend your time and money?

If so, your Realtor or new neighbors should be a source of contacts for repairs and renovations that are beyond your skill set.

Some communities have newsletters or websites where vendors can buy advertising space. Always ask for a copy of the newsletter when you visit the office or homes for sale. You'll find ads for inspectors, plumbers, roof repair, bath and kitchen remodelers and others who specialize in home projects.

Other residents are a preferred source of recommendations, and you'll find most are happy to talk with you about their community and the vendors who typically work there. You'll also find ads in local papers and through online social media sites and Craigslist.

Always check for proper licensing and insurance, and know that requirements vary from place to place.

Popular renovations include the kitchen and bathrooms. These areas are especially susceptible to hidden damage so be prepared for either one to turn into a cascading event that begins with new cabinets and ends with replacing wallboard that has rotted behind the tile, or expensive plumbing leaks before you even start on the cabinetry and fixtures.

When my client Martha decided to remodel the small master bath in her 1980s home, she planned to spend about $3,500 on the project. In addition to a new shower stall, toilet and vanity, she planned to paint the walls and replace the tile flooring.

As the contractor removed the existing fixtures he found some problems. All told, the cost increased from $3,500 to $6,000. Now it's a lovely bathroom that should last for years, but the moral of that story is to be prepared for unexpected issues to arise during a remodeling project.

Also, be sure you're following local permitting guidelines, be they city or county. You may need a licensed contractor and you may need permits, even for something as simple as a new water heater.

If you're interested in a fixer upper or even some light updating, the first item on your to-do list should be to find a good home inspector who understands the area and common construction issues. Also ask your Realtor to bring in a remodeler to help evaluate homes you are serious about.

Although the savings might seem attractive at first glance, I have seen many buyers end up spending just as much fixing up a home as they would have buying a new home or almost new home in the first place.

Heck, I have been one of those buyers, several times. I have also been one of those sellers, and believe me it is painful to look at the bottom line when you have over-improved for the house or the neighborhood.

Again, is this really the way you want to spend your time and money? Remodeling always take longer than it should and costs more than originally estimated, sometimes much, much more.

There is also the personal supervision required, even though you're using a contractor. People have different ideas of good design and aesthetics. Sometimes the person you think would know best has little or no regard for design details.

Have you ever ended up with the towel rack off-center and installed too high for your convenience? You'll see it every time you walk into the room. Or the drapery rod that's not quite level or hung just a tad high or low for your new drapes? Endlessly annoying.

Remodeling is a major commitment of not only your time and your money, but your energy. Consider it from all angles before you set your sights on that bargain house that just needs a little tender loving care to be perfect.

Surprised?

Resistance can pop up from surprising sources. Your own mind is another one, with its constant need for safety and security.

Remember, the brain is wired to maintain

the safe and known status quo, to put it simply. Any new adventure is a threat. That's why it is so helpful to carefully consider all aspects of your coming retirement, work through the exercises, and refer to your goals on a regular basis.

The brain will be somewhat soothed by your proof of concept – the facts, figures, and success stories – that you develop as you move forward. I'm not saying your logical mind will be your biggest source of support, it will still play the Chicken Little theme song at every opportunity.

But you will have tools handy to help you follow the guidance of your heart and soul, instead of your oh-so-fearful amygdala, that primitive part of the brain that equates change with danger and gives rise to the feeling of fear.

But if you slow down a bit, pay attention to the fear and move forward in spite of it, you may find your anxiety transforming into excitement at the prospect of all that awaits you.

And in

Conclusion

You're about to join those 10,000 other Baby Boomers retiring every day. If you're among the 50 percent who plan to move for retirement, you now have a bucket full of information and tools to help you begin the process.

Recognizing that housing is your most significant expense – assuming good health – you are prepared to embark on a mission to find the perfect rightsized place to enjoy the coming 20 to 30 or more years of retirement. Or perhaps semi-retirement if you plan to work part-time or volunteer in your community.

You also realize just how important community and your friends are to your physical health and emotional well-being. And you're dedicated to seeking out relationships that support your next phase of life.

In this book, I revealed the steps to take and the pitfalls to avoid. Through a series of worksheets (which you can download from my website, if you haven't already) you estimated how much money you'll have available in retirement, then created a plan of action.

You have learned the inside scoop on how to sell your home for top dollar and probably been a bit disappointed to learn just how little all your other physical trappings are worth on the open market. You also know more about how to evaluate potential new communities and decide what style of home will work best for you.

By adding this data to your own knowledge and experience, you can move forward with confidence!

Online
Resources

I'm constantly updating and supplementing the information presented in this book. Be sure to visit my website for access to worksheets and other valuable resources like links to the latest articles and studies on the topic of life in retirement.

Find the worksheets at **sonyamyers.com/ insiders**

As you dive deeper into the process of rightsizing, feel free to contact me with your questions or comments via my website. I'm honored to become part of your support network.

Worksheet

Here's one more worksheet you can access on my site at sonyamyers.com/insiders.

Community Worksheet for _____

Features

Age Restricted/55+   ___ Yes ___ No

Gated   ___ Yes ___ No

Guarded   ___ Yes ___ No
    ___ Paid ___ Volunteer

Recreation Building   ___ Yes ___ No
    Activities ___ Yes ___ No
    Access ___ Key ___ Unlocked

Community Pool   ___ Yes ___ No
    Size _____ Heated? ___ Spa? ___

Community Fitness   ___ Yes ___ No
    Included ___ or Extra ___, $_____

    Equipment   ___ Yes ___ No

    Classes   ___ Yes ___ No

    Sports   ___ Tennis
       ___ Pickleball
       ___ Bocce
       ___ Shuffleboard
       ___ Golf

Marina   ___ Yes ___ No
    Included ___ or Extra ___, $_____

HOA Fees $_____ Month/Quarter/Year

Maintenance Fees

    $_____ Month/Quarter/Year

    Includes:

Pets

Pet Restrictions   ___ Yes ___ No
    ___ Fences ___ Number ___ Size

Vehicle Restrictions

Trucks Allowed   ___ Yes ___ No

Motorcycles Allowed   ___ Yes ___ No

Commercial Vehicles   ___ Yes ___ No

RVs Allowed   ___ Yes ___ No

Golf Carts Allowed   ___ Yes ___ No

Boats/Boat Trailers   ___ Yes ___ No

    Storage Lot?   ___ Yes ___ No
    Included ___ or Extra ___, $_____

Must vehicles be parked in garage?
                ___ Yes ___ No

Visitors

Registration required   ___ Yes ___ No

Length of visit restricted ___ Yes ___ No

Youngest age allowed   _____

Maximum number allowed   _____

Rentals

Rentals allowed   ___ Yes ___ No

Approval required   ___ Yes ___ No

Minimum rental period?   _____

How many times per year?   _____

Tenant pets allowed   ___ Yes ___ No

Maximum number occupants _____

Community Worksheet

Information on potential communities is one of the hardest things to keep organized. Here's a sample you can create right now on good old-fashioned paper.

Ask some or all of these questions when you're looking into a development or neighborhood. Once you have identified what is important to you, modify the list to create your own version and use it to keep track of the various communities you're considering.

When working with buyers, I find it helpful to supply them with a clipboard holding copies of listings we're scheduled to see, as well as checklists like the following. Once you have your form, carry it with you while home shopping.

COMMUNITY NAME

Features

55 plus / age restricted

Gated or guarded

  Paid

  Volunteer

Recreation building

  Activities

  Method of Access

Pool

  Size

  Heated

  Spa

Fitness, Free or Extra Cost?

  Equipment

  Classes

Sports

  Tennis

  Pickleball

  Bocce

  Shuffleboard

  Golf

Marina

Other

Pet restrictions

Type

Number

Size

Breeds

Leash laws

Noise

Vehicles

Trucks

Motorcycles

Commercial vehicles

Recreational vehicles

Golf carts

Boats/boat trailers

Visitors

Length of visit

Ages

Number of guests at one time

Approval required

Rental Restrictions

Rent or Lease allowed

Number of times per year

Length of time

Tenant pets

Approval required

Ongoing Costs

HOA fees

Monthly, Quarterly, Annual

Maintenance fees

Monthly, Quarterly, Annual

Miscellaneous

Fences allowed

Landscaping allowed

Distance to shopping

Distance to beach, boating, etc.

A personal invitation

I hope you enjoyed *Downsize Your Home, Rightsize Your Life*. Thank you from the bottom of my heart for reading this book. Writing it was a labor of love and I appreciate your time and attention to the results.

If so inclined, please take a few moments to write a review on Amazon and share your opinion with future readers. Just search for the title or visit your order history. Also, please connect with me via:

My website: sonyamyers.com

Facebook: facebook.com/sonyaBmyers

LinkedIn: linkedin.com/in/sonyamyers

Acknowledgments

The completion of this book would not have been possible without the participation, assistance, and support of the following people:

My husband Bill, who suffered through my many periods of doubt and frustration when the words wouldn't behave themselves.

All my real estate friends, associates, and customers who — although names and details have been changed to protect their privacy — contributed information vital to the effort.

Editor Houkje Ross and technical whiz Maryna Smuts.

Finally, all the high school English teachers who told me I should be a writer. I blame you for this.

Made in the USA
Middletown, DE
18 December 2019

81174119R00085